FAVORITE TOYS

ACTION FIGURES

BY CHRIS BOWMAN

EPIC

BELLWETHER MEDIA · MINNEAPOLIS, MN

EPIC

Action and adventure collide in **EPIC**.
Plunge into a universe of powerful
beasts, hair-raising tales, and high-speed
excitement. Astonishing explorations await.
Can you handle it?

Library of Congress Cataloging-in-Publication Data

LC record for Action Figures available at: https://lccn.loc.gov/2021044264

Editor: Elizabeth Neuenfeldt   Designer: Josh Brink

Printed in the United States of America, North Mankato, MN.

TABLE OF CONTENTS

To The Rescue! 4

The History of 6
Action Figures

Action Figures Today 16

More Than A Toy 20

Glossary 22

To Learn More......................23

Index....................................24

To The Rescue!

The world is in danger. An evil **villain** is trying to take over. The toys are in trouble!

Suddenly, the Avengers appear. They fight the villain. They win! The Avengers action figures saved the day.

The History of Action Figures

G.I. Joe was the first action figure. It was made by Hasbro in 1964.

The toy was around 12 inches (30 centimeters) tall. It could change **poses**. It also had many outfits and **accessories**.

U.S. MARINES G.I. JOE

ACTION FIGURE BEGINNINGS

Hasbro offices, Pawtucket, Rhode Island = ⚪

U.S. NAVY G.I. JOE

U.S. ARMY G.I. JOE

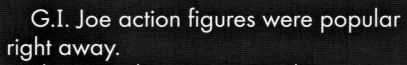

G.I. Joe action figures were popular right away.

The United States was in the **Vietnam War** at the time. Many kids liked G.I. Joe and other **military** toys.

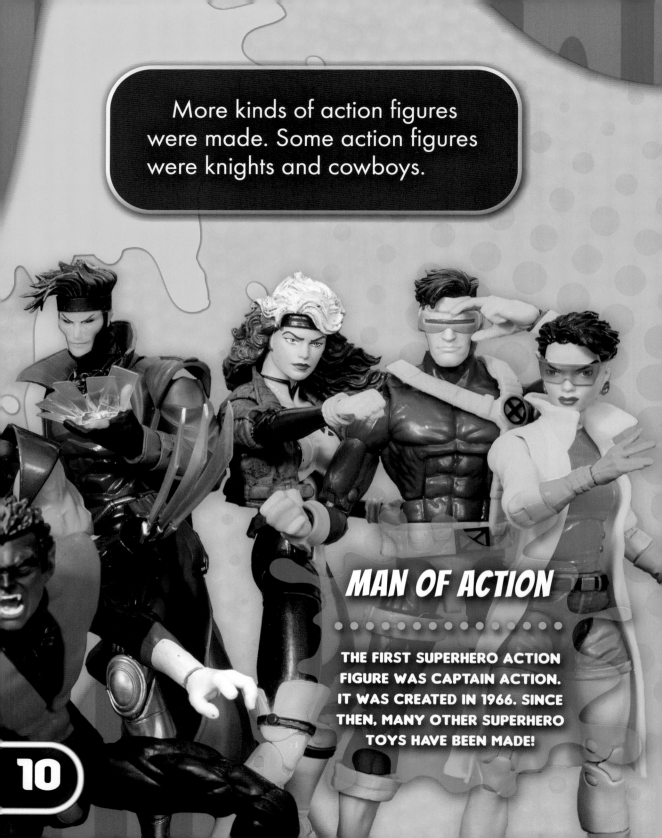

More kinds of action figures were made. Some action figures were knights and cowboys.

MAN OF ACTION

THE FIRST SUPERHERO ACTION FIGURE WAS CAPTAIN ACTION. IT WAS CREATED IN 1966. SINCE THEN, MANY OTHER SUPERHERO TOYS HAVE BEEN MADE!

Other action figures were **astronauts** and superheroes. There were even figures of **spies**!

ACTION MAN
ASTRONAUT

In the 1970s, many action figures became smaller. These were cheaper to make.

STRETCH ARMSTRONG ™

S-T-R-E-T-C-H
HE RETURNS TO NORMAL SIZE!

Contents: 13" Stretch Armstrong Figure

SUPER STRETCHY

STRETCH ARMSTRONG WAS MADE IN 1976. THE FIGURE WAS FILLED WITH GEL AND STRETCHED TO FOUR TIMES ITS ORIGINAL SIZE!

The most popular figures were from Star Wars. They were less than 4 inches (10 centimeters) tall!

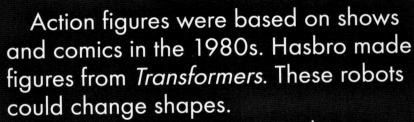

Action figures were based on shows and comics in the 1980s. Hasbro made figures from *Transformers*. These robots could change shapes.

Teenage Mutant Ninja Turtles toys were also popular. Figures were made for **professional wrestlers**, too!

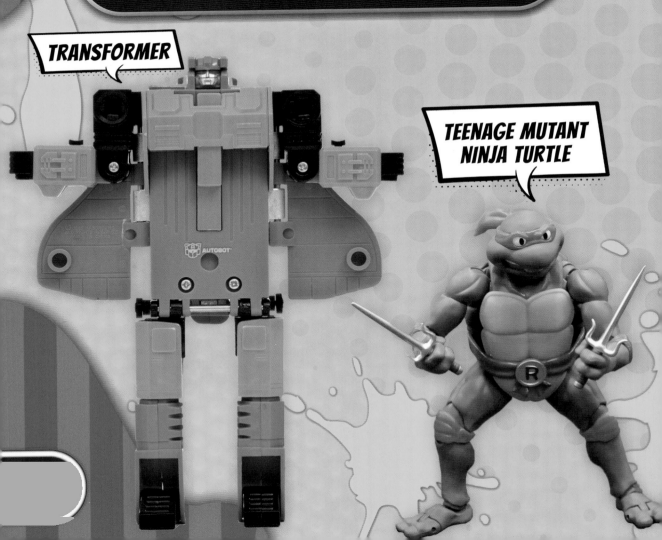

TRANSFORMER

TEENAGE MUTANT NINJA TURTLE

ACTION FIGURE TIMELINE

1964
G.I. Joe is released by Hasbro

1976
Stretch Armstrong figures are released

PROFESSIONAL WRESTLER ACTION FIGURE

1977
Kenner releases the first Star Wars action figures

1984
Hasbro's *Transformers* figures are released

Action Figures Today

Today, Marvel and Star Wars action figure sets are popular. Sets are often made for each new film.

Some sets are based on famous scenes. These figures can be very **detailed**.

MARVEL AVENGERS SET

ACTION FIGURE TYPES

Marvel Comics

Transformers

Star Wars

WWE Wrestling

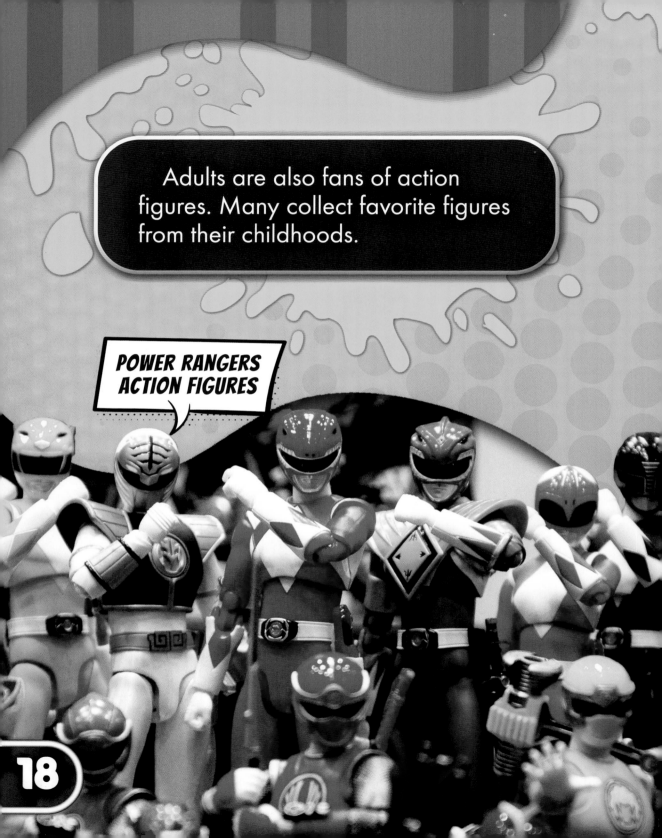

Adults are also fans of action figures. Many collect favorite figures from their childhoods.

POWER RANGERS ACTION FIGURES

No. 38190

PRICE

STAR WARS

KENNER STAR WARS ACTION FIGURE

Princess Leia Organa

Kenner

Some action figures are worth a lot of money. **Rare** figures can cost thousands of dollars!

More Than A Toy

There are many ways to enjoy action figures. Many people learn about their history at museums. Fans also go to action figure **conventions**. Action figures are featured in movies like *Toy Story*. There is an action figure for everyone!

ACTION FIGURE MUSEUM DISPLAY

TOY STORY PROFILE

What Is It? Movie series about toys and action figures

When Did It Start? 1995

How Many Movies Have Been Made? Four, with a spin-off called *Lightyear* coming in 2022

Glossary

accessories—items added to something else to make it more useful or attractive

astronauts—people who are trained to travel in space

conventions—events where fans of a subject meet

detailed—having many small items or parts

military—related to the armed forces

poses—ways of standing

professional wrestlers—people who are paid to wrestle

rare—hard to find

spies—people who secretly gather information

Vietnam War—a war in Southeast Asia that took place from 1955 to 1975; U.S. troops fought in the war from 1965 to 1973.

villain—an evil character

To Learn More

AT THE LIBRARY

Dinmont, Kerry. *Toys and Games Past and Present.* Minneapolis, Minn.: Lerner Publications, 2019.

Higgins, Nadia. *Toys Then and Now.* Minneapolis, Minn.: Jump!, 2019.

Sommer, Nathan. *Barbie Dolls.* Minneapolis, Minn.: Bellwether Media, 2022.

ON THE WEB

FACTSURFER

Factsurfer.com gives you a safe, fun way to find more information.

1. Go to www.factsurfer.com.

2. Enter "action figures" into the search box and click 🔍.

3. Select your book cover to see a list of related content.

Index

astronauts, 11

Avengers, 4, 5, 16

beginnings, 7

Captain Action, 10

collect, 18

comics, 14

conventions, 20

cowboys, 10

G.I. Joe, 6, 7, 8, 9

Hasbro, 6, 14

history, 6, 7, 8, 10, 11, 12, 13, 14, 20

knights, 10

Marvel, 16

museums, 20

professional wrestlers, 14, 15

profile, 21

sets, 16

shows, 14

sizes, 6, 12, 13

spies, 11

Star Wars, 13, 16, 19

Stretch Armstrong, 12

superheroes, 10, 11

Teenage Mutant Ninja Turtles, 14

timeline, 15

Toy Story, 20, 21

Transformers, 14

types, 17

United States, 8

Vietnam War, 8

worth, 19

The images in this book are reproduced through the courtesy of: CTR Photos, front cover (hero); Willrow Hood, front cover (Boba Fett), back cover (Luke Skywalker, G.I. Joe), p. 17 (Star Wars); Ivan_Sabo, front cover (Teenage Mutant Ninja Turtle); Aisyaqilumaranas, front cover (Buzz Lightyear), back cover (Optimus Prime), pp. 2 (Iron Man), 4 (Captain America), 5 (Iron Man), 14 (Teenage Mutant Ninja Turtle), 18, 22; Krikkiat, front cover (Spider-Man), p. 2 (Spider-Man, Hulk), pp. 10, 17 (Spider-Man); VINCENT GIORDANO PHOTO, front cover (soldier); ferdyboy, front cover (Batman); worapon lertprasertwet, back cover (toy soldiers); GOLFX, back cover (Iron Man); KhunO, back cover (Charizard); TheFarAwayKingdom, p. 4 (dinosaur); Stock photo by Yaa, p. 5 (Hulk, child); Justin Sullivan/ Getty Images, pp. 6 (G.I. Joe box), p. 9; Chris Willson/ Alamy, pp. 6 (U.S. Marines G.I. Joe), 7, 12, 15 (G.I. Joe, Stretch Armstrong, Transformer); Mike Groll/ AP Images, p. 8; Shepic/ Alamy, p. 11; CTRPhotos, pp. 13 (all), 17 (wrestling action figure); Marc Tielemans/ Alamy, p. 14 (Transformer); Liam Collins/ Alamy, p. 15 (wrestling action figure); phol_66, p. 16; Andy Beckett/ Alamy, p. 17 (Transformer); benstoybarn/ Alamy, p. 19; Image Vault/ Alamy, p. 20; Christian Bertrand, p. 21 (Toy Story logo); All Star Picture Library/ Alamy, p. 21; FUN FUN PHOTO, p. 23.